Dedication

Perry, Thank you for your support of my words and my heart.

Julian, thank you for showing me love can materialize into greatness! You are mommy's inspiration ☺

Brandon, your strength and integrity is what I admire most about you. I hope to maintain that truth in your life.

Nina, you are the best of God's gift's-I love you

Mom, thank you for encouraging me to take my writing to another level

To my girlfriends who have shared their highs and lows-you are heard

Contents

Ambient Passion

Body and Soul

FROM A DISTANCE

I do not hate but I dislike hearing, "I've got to go" or anything that has to deal with you leaving

OOPS! There goes my selfish trait again! Wanting to have you to myself, wanting you to stay by my side, wanting you to be there when I get off work to hold me or for me to tell you how my day has been

When I am with you I feel at total peace

The day that you leave I feel so many mixed emotions

I miss you so much

I cannot explain or show you how much I love you

I cannot explain or show how happy I am to have found the courage to tell you how I felt about you, you mean so much to me, you are so important to me

I feel that you are a part of me and without you here I feel like a half person, I half smile

I do not mean to have an attitude if I show it; it is not meant to show, but when you say, "I've got to hit the road" I cringe. I can no longer stand the distance between us yet I will bear the miles to be with you even for a day

I can no longer take the phone calls yet I will call every hour if that is what it takes
I feel lonely when you leave,

I feel anger when you leave,

I cry when you leave,

I feel anxiety when you leave,

Is this a crime to feel the way I do?

MISSING

It has been said time and time again, men are good for nothin' but good for somethin'

I am in need of a man now, not for anything sexual but for a certain amount of intimacy

Yeah, that is what I am missing now

Just to be held while the only sound is good jazz and/or our heartbeats in unison

I am lonely now

Lonely to look at someone and to kiss him because I feel like it, to have his arm around me, kiss my hair, forehead

To tell me how beautiful I am, how sexy my lips are, how my eyes dance, how smooth my skin is, how pretty my smile is

I just want to close my eyes and lay back in the strength of his chest and legs

I am lonely now

For a sensual body to roll over and kiss and bury my head in the hairs of his chest with our legs tangled, bodies in sync

Damn I am longing to be touched, massaged, cooed over....

I am cold and cannot seem to get warmed by an empty tub, gas heat

ONE IS A LONELY NUMBER

On a lonely evening, in a lonely home, in the corner is that lonely girl with a lonely heart

Wine cannot warm up her soul, hot chocolate can help only for a minute the soul is so cold the liquid cools at the mouth

I am searching…

Searching for the passion, rhythm that moves my hips

It is hard to dance in front of a mirror

I would rather dance for you, at least there is a reaction, not just myself staring in an empty mirror or me turning off the radio and going to bed sleeping the lonely hours away

I am a beautiful woman with much love, passion, power to give
It is hard to find a partner who would like just that but it always has to lead to sex then all the passion built up is regurgitated along with the sensuality
Sex deprives all the afore mentioned-especially when the lovin' is good it always has to end, leading to disappointment and regret
Sex is too deep, too intimate, too close to the soul
It just messes up everything!!
I just want to wear my negligee's, walk barefoot, without having to take them off and be violated by the quickness of an unnecessary romp which always ruins the ambiance of passion.

DEAR SOMEONE

Why do I still miss you? Why do certain songs bring me floating to your soul?

You and I know you did me a big favor but I still long for you.

First loves are hard to get over, no matter how much they disrespect,

use,

and mistreat you. I still think of you.
I am over you
       YET
I still love you
When I think of wine, candles & romance
There you are.
Feeling a summer breeze flow over my body & the warm yet cools sensation fill me and….
There you are.
When I come home and prepare a meal
There you are.
Taking a bubble bath; as I let the bubbles flow down my back-I slide down, I look up and….
There you are.
Sometimes I feel the touch of another & I think of you.
Riding along someone on a new journey, you're there.
Tossing & turning through the night
Our nude bodies are intertwined.
Cuddling with a good book, jazz on, wine glass near
I'm in your domain

On dull winter days
I walk with your arms around me

On the Flipside

I am glad you are gone.
You were beginning to change & I began to not like you
anymore.
Your attitude about things were on a minute scale
Even though I forgave the infidelity I knew
It was beneath me & you knew too.

All and All

I miss you
you were like a fun girlfriend
maybe more than a betrayer of feelings
Now I hide emotions actually I have none of
the "love" type
The urge to trust is erased
The want to love has a bitter taste
The need to make love is an act of repulsion
for one to touch my hand, caress my face, hug me leaves
me much to be desired.

Dear someone,
I know you're there.
Dear someone,
Did you really care?
Dear someone,

Life is better off
Dear someone,
I can't believe I actually wanted spend a lifetime as your
partner. Believe me I never
felt that strong for anyone
but I never let anyone into my heart as you.
I guess the thrill was the chase
keeping my guard up (and I was serious!)
& letting you in on a chance
that was blown.

Dear someone,
I am over you
but something won't let you go.
I don't remember your face
I don't remember most things
I remember the first person I met
I remember the real person that was romantic
I remember the right way it should have been

Dear someone.

Across a crowded café

Chocolate

             Cinnamon

Mocha

          Spice

      The middle of a coffeehouse and I felt nice

Do you ever have the feeling of eyes burning your chest?

      It is a good feeling I must confess to know someone
is staring at my breast!

It is a sunny day in June and I am leaving soon.
                And then I
notice you across the crowded room
I knew you once as you glance my way
                  I wonder if you are
here alone so I'll have a good day
Your partner joins, **he** I am glad to see
                But Oh! How
I long for it to be me!
I push away feelings I can't hide
                I pray to the
Lord to be my guide
You look as if unsure, should you speak?

      But I am sure the way I look at you and glance
      unknowingly, my face thoughtless, you
      ask your friend and the man upstairs of my
      acceptance you still seek

The feelings coming over me of wanting to kiss you so bad

                                        All our stay
we glance across
You checking me out

                                        Me checking
you out
Games over

                                        We're done
Coffee break is over

                                        We both look
discouraged
We want to speak, touch each other one more time
                                        Before we go
on with our week
You can't go on, someone should talk

                              At least I know one
spot where you are weak
You have to speak to me, to see if there is an inkling if it is
still you I seek

                                        I straighten up
as you approach
I squint to see that God forsaken broach!

          We hug and you kiss my cheek. We look into each
other's eyes and quickly sit
Saying less than 10 words and that is it
                                        We spoke to
each other as strangers
We both long for more

                                        But the fear of
rejection is a feeling hard to ignore
The days go on as usual

                                        I miss you
You miss me

But I will

faintly remember that day
I saw you across that crowded café

CONTEMPLATIONS

I DREAM OF ZIMBABWE:
Unending horizon, open land, tropical warmth, dancing
around me
I DREAM OF YOU:
Café au lait
smooth
gentle
shy
gorgeous
innocent
real
trusting
unlike no other
I DREAM OF LOVE:
uplifting
happiness
perfection
blue skies and butterflies
feet never touching the ground
I FEEL LUST:
passion
fire
thunderstorms
tenderness
I FEEL YOUR TOUCH:
Goosebumps
giggles
questions
I LOOK INTO YOUR EYES:
I see us fitting together like puzzle pieces

I see forever
I see me
I see passion
I see shyness
Unspoken words and desires
I WANT YOU:
to speak to me
to know me
to let down any inhibition
to take a deep breath and tell me, what is your name? your
aim?
how do you feel about me and what do you want to do
about it?
I SEE:
us talking, laughing and enjoying every moment
I see people envying us because we stare at each other in
our own world
because we knew from the start that the other belonged in
the others heart

YOU LEFT YOUR RADIO ON

What does one need in order to let go?
Perhaps memories to be erased?
A hypnotist?
Deep subconsciously so there will be no trace?
Music, sweet music to caress the night
Fears
Lost lovemaking
Breathless
I am breathless
Am I blue?
Melancholy?
Blind to realism
Is fantasy the only answer to problems?
I am longing for a touch of you…..to smell your….feel you
I need to feel you so bad
I can no longer dream of wishful fantasies
I want to taste you and have you taste me
I long to have you near, the rhythms of my heart has beaten
you out yet you grip my heart
Just by a glance   squeezing   choking
I am blue
Why can I not stop thinking of you?
I hate you
      NO
You hate me
      NO
How can you long, live, love someone that does not want to
be with you?

Who is not man enough to stand up, you cannot stand up to
yourself
I am drowning
You are down on me
In me
I am trying to push you out and I cannot breathe
I am blue, are you?
What makes this so different? I can let go easily but this
grip keeps getting tighter and tighter my eyes hurt, my
chest
I have collapsed on the red carpet of love
That damn music is playing
I am eroticated   toxicated   nauseated
I am tired of rolling over and staring at darkness..........

JAZZ

What is it about JAZZ music I love?
Is it because of the silent words conveyed?
Not of degradation or the hint of sexual excursions.
JAZZ speaks of gentleness, whatever you want it to be.
For me it is a peaceful calm,
                eroticism,
                a journey to a place outside myself,
                my closest friend,
                the ease of a road trip,
                true,
                a message longed to be heard.
The sound of instrumentation:
        The sax has a way of undressing my soul and
making my hips sway to a lustful rhythm.
        The piano tickles my erotic fantasies and the rhythm
permeates my soul to my fingertips.
        The keys add a joyful thrust to my listening sending
me on a journey
where I am free from interruptions, pressures
so it can speak to me,
move me
groove me
do me
Is shouting aloud?

Venus De Milo

Hello Venus
How are you?
There alone with no one to do

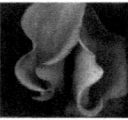Oh! I am doing o.k.
Feeling a little lonely
Changing scenes is the thing here lately

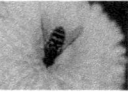No one has come to see you? I am really
surprised
You are so beautiful everyone who meets you falls in love

Yeah well, I am on a little retreat trying to find
myself and find a special someone who can come and
visit me whenever he pleases

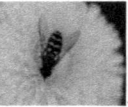So no one is seeing you? How do you feel?

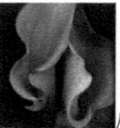Most days are dark, most nights are dark

Yeah you look pale to me and your hair is a bit overgrown

You never miss your water until your well runs dry and even in the rainy season I have had drought

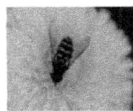
Venus, someone will soon come along and you will be pretty, tight and vibrant all over again. Just make sure your guest will protect you, respect you and never neglect you. You are the most important woman who is hard to please. But when you are happy you spread yourself so...huggin' men so tight they do not want to let go.

Gee thanks, you are making me blush...just don't stare at me I did not say hush!

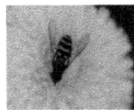
Venus oh Venus, there is a cruel world between us

And sometimes I just dream of a nice warm penis and nothing but moist air between us

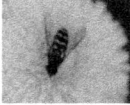

May I?

You may not! I have overstepped my bounds and got you all hot

It is not you it is me. I know you have been alone and I was trying to see....

Buzz off my friend!

I TASTED YOU FOR THE FIRST TIME

I went down on you for a special occasion-I just felt like it

I watched you walking around naked and your penis looked so delicious I just had to have a taste!

You brought him to me and I engulfed it! My vagina throbbed as you bobbed your dick in & out my mouth

You grooved your hips to my uvula

It went so deep I thought I saw stars

So deep I opened my eyes to find my lashes tangled in your hairs and tickling my nose

As I watched your hips thrust & my head agrees trying to keep up to your rhythm

I wish I had a recorder to watch our synchronous motion

Damn you look good as you bite your lip enjoying me sucking your righteousness....

Let me lick there again to make you move that way 1 more time-dance baby dance…

I have never seen a man's nipples that erect

I've learned a couple of new things here: you can fuck me in the mouth, you can make moves like a dancer and sounds only a puppy could make when my mouth is controlling your head

All I want to know is how can I discreetly spit out the seeds?

SNACK BOX

My lips taste like gingerbread

My neck a ring of licorice

My nipples fruity gum balls

and you lick and lick and lick

My back a sheet of butter rum cake

My ass a Bundt of lemon

You part my legs as your mouth dives into my decadent
truffle

and you thrust and thrust and thrust

Drippings of icing and nibbling my butterscotch ankles

as the volcano of sweetness churns and churns

I erupt a melody of crimson praline

Auto-Pilot

Goodness comes but once a year
I don't ask questions but thank the Lord over and over
For what I assume is the G spot exploding, humming and
throbbing.

"that's the spot"

I know it is the reason why women jab vibrators into
themselves

"get me hot"

…the reason why some float from dick to dick searchin' for
a little mo' G rubbin' those slender fingers cannot bring

"make me happy"

I am lucky…I can dream a dream and awake to that
throbbing goodness starting from the pit of my stomach to
the tips of my toes or tense as my lover turns me to my
stomach-- I press my hips down and he pumps my pussy
for information and my heart races and races and my breath
escapes me, my gums tingle and I scream for Mercy as my
clitoris becomes the size of a full water balloon full of
power and might. I pray I don't pass out or scream like a
werewolf

"Don't stop"

there goes my vision and my baby yelling, "damn!" while I
flood over his balls, thighs, stomach....my nails ripping the
sheets as I shake and I am done. This is when I wish I could

do this solo 'cuz now I have to wait for him to cum and finish.

Just me, myself and thigh

the throb is getting slower and slower
this feels so damned good!!!
I love a good fuck beat down or when I am awakened by knock…knock…knock on the ocean of ecstasies door I cross my legs and squeeze and am again paralyzed by the best feeling in the world!!
caramel being squeezed out of a chocolate bar, electricity, will I die from not breathing and my heart beating hard like that?
 the feeling purges the depths of my soul and I sound like a cow with a pillow over its face
hips don't fail me now as I almost become 1 with the mattress and go into the twilight

I am on fire

Sheets soaking wet as our bodies sing a melody of slappin' sweatiness, funk, desire, hunger

I'll see you again in a couple of months around 3:42 or 5:45 a.m. either some obnoxious dream will awake me subconsciously or my lovers dick will curve over and pet my clit so that I will again see stars, speak in a cosmic tongue before I lose connectivity pray the waves will not overtake me with such a thunderous rush as it did before and before and before and before….

Segue to a fantasy

Sweet love nectar

Honey lips

Peppermint hips

Auras of chocolate

Melodies of musk

As your love engulfs me

the sweetness melts between my breasts…..

A FANTASY OF WHAT'S TO COME

Thursday July19

I received a letter with no return address. Who's sending me something? I open it as I walk down the hallway. Hmm…it is an invitation:

> YOU ARE INVITED TO THE NIGHT
> OF YOUR DREAMS:
> THE ATHENIUM
> SUITE 1015
> 555 BRUSH
> DETROIT 7:00 7-21-20XX
> B.Y.B.B *BRING YOUR BEAUTIFUL
> BODY -X

X? Who is X? Well, whoever has me aroused for as I opened the invitation rose petals fell onto me. The envelope has the scent of CK One.

He knows me.

Back to X. Every guy I know knows CK One is the only scent that leads me to shore and of course I'm a pushover for roses.

Should I go out to purchase a negligee? Who am I dating now? Too bad it isn't my crush sending this.

2 days.

Friday July 20

I've been checking my answering machine all day. No suspicious calls.

Saturday July 21

I've narrowed it down to who I want it to be, who I
hope it isn't and well…someone I'll tolerate.
Do I want go? Yes! but I hate this mysterious stuff. It's
5:00 I guess I should get movin'
I'll pack my Louis Vuitton overnighter
I'll shower with my fave scent; wear my Vickie's Secret
lace red bra, panties and garter. I'll wear my short skirt and
'come and get me' blouse.

      6:30 I'm on my way to play with dream lover
      I've got to roll the window down, my arms are
sweatin', butterflies a twirlin'…
      I'm here…my legs are wobblin' to the elevator and
I am looking around the lobby for a clue but there is no
one.
      Room 1015. Corner suite, I'm impressed!

      There is a note sticking underneath the door:
      HELLO BEAUTIFUL, HERE'S THE KEY
      LET YOURSELF IN & ENJOY! –O

      I'm trying not to grin from ear to ear as I open the
door and see red and pink roses about the room. There are
candles leading from the living room to the bedroom with
sticky notes telling me which piece of clothing to take off.
      THE RIVER IS BEGINNING TO GET A LITTLE
      TURBULENT
      I didn't know there was a fireplace in here
      THE DAM IS LOSING ITS STRUCTURE

      PRESS PLAY
      XO

Coltrane   Yes I know who; it is you dream lover

There is a quilt on the floor with champagne, fruit and other food toys.

I'm scared to turn around-I feel the heat

"Hello"

My heart stops. I turn in what seems like slow motion and see a bronze body staring at me.

He's dressed in red boxers and a matching robe.

I lust you.

As I open my mouth to say hello I am instructed to keep quiet and to just…………. FEEL

I am now blind folded and only wearing underclothes

I can feel him moving close to me for he has on my favorite scent

I feel something on my mouth

"DRINK"

I take a sip of champagne; it sends tingles all over me

"OPEN"

I taste melon in my mouth, the juices flow over my lips as a kiss dries them

"I'VE MISSED YOU"

He says as he removes the blindfold and embraces me as if I've been lost. I run my fingers through his wavy locks.

We part and I gaze into his brown eyes.

Damn this man is sexy!

He takes a long piece of melon puts ½ in his mouth and we both nibble then kiss each other deeply. His mouth is moist; his skin is as soft as a baby's bottom. I don't want this kiss to end because Lord knows what I may do. I can't help but to moan.

SHUT UP!!!

we part and I wait to catch my breath. He cups my face in his hands, stares into my eyes and we both stand together as

if we are puppets on a string and we begin to move to the
jazz rhythms together. My goose bumps make me shiver
and I press my chest deeper into his, I love the curly hair on
his chest, I bury my head into his shoulders and inhale
  I feel his breath upon my ear
  Feel his hand slide down my back
beginning at the shoulders
down the side to my lower spine
he wraps his arms around me tighter and I feel my breath
going quickly
      THE DAMN IS BROKEN
AND WILL SOON OVERFLOW
We do sort of a 'nae nae', butterfly move and we part with
laughter, nervous laughter as I eye his penis
  He leads me up the stairs to the tub where a steamy
bath is waiting
He lights the candles and I look around to see a bevy of
bubbles waiting for me
I smile and again open my mouth to speak but a kiss hushes
me again. I wonder how soon the water will cool when I
get my goose bumps in the tub.
   There is so much I want to say well, actually do
My bra is soon unsnapped before I know it
  I stand cold
As he stares and kisses each nipple
I tremble and wobble to the other side then throw a glance,
with the music still playing I catch the unfamiliar rhythm
and begin to sway, then again turn to catch his eye
         and his
penis staring
  my mouth begins to water.

As I let the underlying rhythm move my hips I release my garter then stand with my arms crossed against my breast

I've heard people can tell what I'm thinking just by looking at me so I thought to myself:

This is going to be a great evening

I'm going to fuck your brains out then

Love you back together

I'm gonna climb all over your body and lick you all over

We'll explore new fantasies together, all inhibitions will be gone

I guess he got the hint because he sexily grinned and came over to me but I put out my arms to stop him and I wiggled my hips and ran to the tub then I slowly turned moving my slow so he could watch me from the back as I gently removed my thong bikini, tossed them at him and slid into the tub.

I giggled watching him stand there with my thong on his face

I won't speak because I sorta like this nonverbal thing we got going on. He finally lets the underwear drop and walks over to the tub. There is a silk drawstring pouch next to the tub-he fumbles in it and pulls out a sponge and bath oils.

Ummmmm.... the water feels good going down my back, I look at him then the water as to say "join me" and he does

I anxiously await the removal of the boxers and my mouth waters again

His body is nice; slim, golden and plain gorgeous! Toned especially the arms, shoulders and those legs-I can just picture those muscles as he pumps me slowly, rhythmically and infinitely....

God IS a good God
His penis a rod
I'm trying not to stare
but I can't   my eyes are watering as
I watch it submerge into the bathtub
The oil is warm as he pours it down my back and I grab a bottle and pour some down his and rub his smooth skin
        I explore his upper body with my eyes, everything is so perfect!
Just like his mind.
Not to rush but I'd like to get out of here and see the rest of his body and lay in his arms and just enjoy
this...
.... moment!!
To move any further would run the ambiance plus absence makes the passion grow fonder!!
        We walk holding hands then he grabs my waist as we past the mirrored closets and our bodies glisten.
                                        We look good together
        We step down into the boudoir of amour and
My body tightens staring at the undone
bed...

PASS THROUGH

The past holds me tight

Like the handcuffs that held me in the bedroom as you loved me

I try to bury it in my memory

But a touch, a smell, a phrase

Will unlock the chains

As my subconscious turns the corner....

I just wanna fuck

Sometimes I just wanna be raw

Not the mother, sister, church-goer, wife

I wanna be a raw vixen with my heels, feathers and cuffs in the mix and we can't forget the tingle me lotion   be naked just fuck

I want you to lay there with your amour ready for me to buff until you come so hard you see white

I don't want cuddle talk

No massages

No niceties

All I want to see is blackness

 matter of factness

Nothing but breaths, body slappin', mattress crackin', moist heat and nothin' neat

If the head board is not hitting the walls, then you aren't banging me hard enough

I want my pussy jammed to the rim with all you have to offer, balls slapping my ass until I am brewing percolator style with cum for you to get intoxicant off of

Round 2, 3, 4...flip, slip, lick, slide, intertwine, stare, smile, clap, slap, pout, wet, sweat

Uninhibited, hair sweated out, make up gone, heels broke, mattress hanging to the right, ceiling fan on blast

I want to light a cigarette when I am done

I want to see indentations on my ass in the morning, a spankin' ain't a spankin' unless the print is there, candle wax flaking off my shoulder, breast so tender I can't wear a bra

I want to sit down really careful like, my lips aching from biting

I want to smell the residue of you on my hands

I want to use the restroom and get a charge from the sweetest pain from our fuck making

I want to wake to the funk of oils, musk, hyacinth

of ass permeating the sheets and walls while Meshell & Marcus are still playing the funk off the bass in the background

How many ways can I tell you I love you?

I love you so much it is indescribable
There are so many things I love about you
I am sure you have no clue
It does not take a rocket scientist to see I love you for you
I love you externally
your pale "Bedrock" feet
your strong hands, your hands tell the story of your life-
rough and hard yet gentle
your eyes are incredibly sexy; I can see the depth of your
soul
your "Kaiser" bun tushy is as cute as a button
your long sexy eyelashes and smooth skin even your little
smile, the gap just adds to the boldness of your sexy face
strong arms to shield me from the cold of this world, chest
to cushion my falls and an embrace to make me feel safe
Internally there is the fear of a child yet there is strength of
a giant
Some insecurity with the security of a mother's embrace
Gentleness, wanting, needing, understanding
Courage let it be told, a heart very bold
When you are gone this tiny place feels like a mansion
I feel alone without my partner
The night is a special time for lovers like you and I
Warm summer nights with clear skies and a blanket of
stars…
The night whispers passion and ideas of romance and
sensuality

Just like our bodies in sync
I love all of you
I think you need to know that

Toe Jam

You must be magic!!

You made me see light in a room full of darkness…

As you softly made love to me

You lifted my legs to the stars

And sucked my toes

You made me a mute!

I recalled my friend telling me, "*Gurl! Don't knock it until you try it; such and such sucked my toes and it felt so good!!*"

I remembered looking at her and thinking "you have lost your fucking mind" "yuk" she stared back with that look on her face that beamed 'good to the last drop' and she was right!

When you did it I could see the whole room even though it was dark my eyes opened so wide along with my mouth from shock! I could not believe this toe seduction!

This little piggy made my eyes roll back-

This little piggy made my pussy gush-

This little piggy made me lose my breath-

How do you like your eggs daddy??

Pucker

I knew you but had no clue about you
of the smoldering flame I never thought could be
my acquaintance then my friend then my confidante
and I still did not know my heart flowed for you
you left and I had feelings of sadness
why?
for years a romance simmered
unknowing
denying
then as a coconut falls and its juices burst
our romance began with one kiss

After work cool down

Mini muffins

Assorted cookies

Heated beverage

Soft music

You

Me

Leather couch

Facing each other with books in our hands

Silence

As we enjoy our favorite past time

Newlyweds

In unison

Toes touching

Passion building

Conversation flowing

Birds chirping

Embers glowing

Me

You

One

Mr. Bubbles

Another Sunday bubble bath alone enveloped with thoughts of you.

Would you like to join me?

Even though you are far away?

I'll pretend my hand is yours

It's dark with nothing but the flicker of a single flame

and the radio

and Wayman Tisdale dealing with Circumstances

Joe-singing my fantasies: 'making love on a beach of jet black sand,

    Out in the rain,
    All night,
    Touching you in places one
would not and some you never knew would get you hot?'

I didn't hear you

Ooh-mmm?

That translates into touch me

Shall I?

Start with my lips and you say do what?

Suck them as I would you

O.K.

Imagine me.

A tub of bubbles with candlelight in my eyes and my jaw motion.

Imagine you –watching

It's hot in here and I've sweat beads on my shoulders, but nothing will stop my sucking…I can taste you salty, warm, Cajun.

My fingers slides pass my bottom lip glistening

as I do some Soulful Moanin'

I slowly rise and arch my back and close my eyes, head tilted as "your" hands massage my breast, "your" hot tongue flicking around my hard nipples standing at attention for you.

(excuse my low guttural moans, the water feels good and……so do you)
Another song that reminds me of you, it's so fitting "Get Me Off"

        "Lovin' is tight
        Can do you all night
        Get ready when I walk through the
door
        Take me and lay me down, kiss me
slow
        from my head to my toes
        Foreplay is all good
        …all I want to say to you baby is get
me off"

I laugh as I think of that leaning back, bringing my legs up, closing my eyes as I feel you get me off

You can't see what I'm doing but my facial expression tells you that I like how you do it

Your wish is my fingers command and my full clit is your audience.

I can't seem to keep my mouth closed and I have to slide down and open wide and take all of you in.

I hate it when I grind my teeth!

I shiver as you purge deeper into my inner being.

I can't breathe as I gaze over at the ½ burned candle

sweat on my face

I'm biting my lip as you move yourself around my lips,
against my clit.

Aphrodite is hummin'cummin' at ya!

I brace…my breath has escaped me!!

    "I give you my wet hands
     I give you the lost map to my bed
     I give you my tapering thighs which are two
slender candles joining in flame
     I give you the power to touch fire
     I give you my waist to encircle with the jewels of
your kisses
     I give you this fragrant entrance
     I give you the hurricane of my orgasm
     I give you the evidence of the ocean in
"Aphrodite"
     I give you back all that you give me
     I give you this, I give you this." *

Anita Endrezze

A segue

In the midst of daily chaos and confusion
I find you like a port in a storm
Your love wraps around me and envelopes my heart
I find joy in your laughter
Safety in your arms
Peace in the melody of your voice

I love you because

I LOVE YOU BECAUSE
You gave me the reality of a beautiful relationship
You give me the courage to better myself

I LOVE YOU BECAUSE
You are honest with me
You genuinely care about me and my well being

I LOVE YOU BECAUSE
You listen to me
You walk beside me
You hold my head up even when I want it to be down (in my funks☺)

I LOVE YOU BECAUSE
You laugh with me
-at me

I LOVE YOU BECAUSE
You had enough heart to say,
"wanna get a room?"

On this day designed to celebrate love, I want to tell you I love you-because

Yearning for the past

I wanna love you like chocolate loves milk
Like black folk love spaghetti and wings
But I can't

I want to feel your skin against my walls, all warm and
funky as the cover gets caught between our legs
I want to our legs to intertwine, want to hear your breath,
moan and feel your tongue caresssssss the back of my neck
But I can't seem to get there

I need help
I need simplicity
I need to really feel loved, not by horny words but by acts
of passion, wordless romance.
You asked me how to be a romantic

Why not do it, be it-romantic in your sense of romance not
what I imagine?

Then my rose may bloom
My eyes will light up and not gaze over as you speak your
passions
I may not feel like they are empty words-if I feel it is your
truth

I wanna love you like I love bass to my Coletrain
Like a baby to a breast
Like I used to for you

Imagine

Imagine

yourself alone to do what you please…

Imagine

you are rubbing me down with oils and treasures…

Imagine

sleeping spoons of you and I…

Imagine

kisses until you are breathless….

Imagine

learning new and more interesting things about the world, about you and me together

Imagine

your sweet nectar extinguishing my burning flame….

Imagine

looking down the V of an arched tigress with honey on her breast….

Imagine

your hands on my wet back as I pant and you stroke…..

Imagine

our chorus of love as we collapse upon a bed of clouds…

Imagine

       staying like that and staring at the stars…

       naked, outside on a blanket of clouds

       with tears in our eyes not knowing why

Imagine

Nowhere to run to

I want to run away but I have nowhere to hide

I want to run away from you, your love has taken my pride

I want to run to find myself, to pull my head out this anthill called love

I've been smothered and gave my last limb

I am unhappy and need it no more

I don't want to talk to you because I blame you—you put yourself out there like that then complained

Quit trying to please them, you need to please me and believe me-I am not pleased!

Hammock Love

I'm free from analytical bondage

Free from worries of abandonment

Free to love

Free to say 'we' instead of me

Free to laugh without abandon, lay where I may

I listen to the rhythm of your voice, it soothes me, like a cashmere blanket

I swim in the laugh of you

Dive in the heat of you

Good for me-true-the love of you

Vivacity

I feel free

I am dancing in circles of my entity

The wind blows my skirt as I dance to the rhythm barefoot

My hips enchanted by the strings and my smile a mile wide

My belly undulates

My sun and moon lengthens and snakes to my percussion

My hair is blowin' in my face as I step, step to the keys of serenity

The way it makes me feel when I think of you

I am at my happy place

At the water, on the pier skipping to your horn with the city as my backdrop and no one but me in your solo

In your eyes I see me twirling arms open wide as I am free in my serenade

Telle est la vie

Such is life

PASS THE P'S

(for Pore)

Friends are fucks
People who sucks
Your vulnerability
Like trucks running over a squirrel
Turns a blind ear to what you hold near and dear
Drains your mind for thoughts they turn inward
Using strengths gained to wane your brain
We are brothers they say as their vampire canines
Suck away at your carotid
Bite into your vein of knowledge and
Cause your heart pain as your blood boils into your
eyes
They put on another disguise to fool another friend
You are left with empty pockets
Laughable conversations
One sided feelings from giving
and giving
and giving
and giving
You are mad, upset, blinded by your own niceties
And wondering, "What the…?"
Fuck him, who needs him
The world goes 'round without you but I have only one
thought for you my friend…
FUCK YOU

VIOLATIONS

I cannot say, "Take off your clothes."
I come up with phrases to get my kids to get ready for bed
or to change their outfits
But I shudder every time "take your close off" slips from
my lips
One violation has caused annihilation in my language

The trauma of this stranger lives on
Someone whom I do not know and words still echo in my
mind
One violent night
Leaves simple that I fight
Music I loved I cannot listen to
Without a river of tears overflowing from my heart

I am a strong woman for facing this trial and putting you in
your place even though
I never knew the sight of your face. I am a 10 and you are a
0
I am a victim's hero but I still cannot say four simple words
that should be easy to relay
Thank God that is all I can
remember...

FEAR OF DEATH

In a world of solemn darkness
I sit and listen to the birds
and swallow a pill of regret.

I see myself 8 feet under
reaching for the sky
looking into blue nothingness
for the answer to my whys.

I stand on top looking at that gaping hole
that goes so deep-jet blackness
I think about a jump but never will
I'm too good for that
but I am glad you are there
up here you would have caused people to jump
into that hole, already living in it unbeknownst.

This stirring of darkness had got me wound tighter then a
wire in a baby grand
tighter than giving a speech in front of hundreds, tighter
than facing myself as I wake in the wee hours in the
morn...
staring at darkness
waiting for lightness
so I can feel rightness
and righteous for both of us

Hormonal wave

It is not time for my period so why am I cryin'?

Tears rising faster than beach tides

At the thought of emptiness, anger

One minute I am folding laundry

Next minute I am tearing up with the memory of you singing, "I love the Lord…I love the Lord…HE is so goooood, HE is so good…"

I see your cocoa brown face playing the piano and your heavy foot tapping the floor

I miss you singing in the car, on the phone, in the living room

You helped me rise to that other level of loving the lord and loving me through him

Your battle with Alzheimer's tore a hole in my heart

Memories I cherish and yearn for

Your long grey hair in pin curls before bed, your worn moo moos, your glasses, pearly smile and your bottom tooth that protruded an inch or so, your loving warm arthritic hands taught me to wrap the Lord's love around me

I cry because my brother came to visit and couldn't stay. The confine of debt and a controlling distrustful love makes all his stays short. I see him walking to the terminal on his way home. His home, a place I'd like to visit but don't feel welcome to enter.

I want to pick up the phone to call my Uncle Pete. I always felt like a little girl when I heard him jump at my voice and ask "how is my little girl?" "How is my little baby?" as he told me stories of his navy days, drinking tequila and I remember his apartment filled with gag trinkets and kinky pens and old man gadgets. I miss the smell of his cologne and his Old Granddad. I miss taking him shopping for Bally shoes and playing Dominoes and his pancakes and baked bacon.

Memories of places I lived and long to be back too.

My period was 2 weeks ago but anger can eclipse my mood in 3 seconds flat!

Now I am angry because I hate you! Your birthday came and you had the nerve to give me a nightmare. I know I have to forgive you to move on but you can't erase years of hate on a whim. I hate you for the rage that lives in me!!

Then I cry

Why?

I want to be quiet with a glass of wine while I have an hour long conversation with my mom, great aunt, my husband or just sitting with my brother.

I am feeling settled right now, grey skies are moving in, the washer is going, my baby boy is at the foot of the bed asking me a stream line of questions and I am in my world of words.

I am lying here and my eyes are tearing

But I have nothing on my mind

Then I Cry-Why?

POTENTIALITY

I start before I finish.
I search but I am lost.
I seek but lose interest in the find.
Do I choose this path for myself?
Do I set myself up to lose?
Everyone sees my light, my star rise, my potential
I start and let it simmer and simmer and simmer…
And I turn the fire off and let my potential marinate and
when the interest arises in me- I have no hunger.
I feel repelled at my potential, my light still shines but I
cannot see it and the cycle begins again.
I start before I can finish.
I seek but never find…

Did the dream die before it was realized?
The past holds a set of keys to the door of my future but I
am held prisoner
of your mistakes.
You tried to guide me but hindered me.
You tried to shield me from what is dangerous but I am a
danger to myself.
I won't let me-be-me-through-me-REALIZE me.
I see but stop before I can be.
I am not me.
I am still simmering, simmering
I found me but lost me.
You never gave me the wings to fly. I lift but dive. I fall
inward.
I need to turn up the fire in me and let myself flow like lava
onto this world
and make my mark for myself if for no one else.
If I don't live to the fullest potential how can anyone else
recognize?

Finish what you start.
Seek and you shall find.
Love and you will be loved.
Accept yourself so others will.
Find love and accept your difference
 make it who you are!

Stagnant

Where do I begin?

How does it end?

The future is uncertain

All I know is today is a bitch

And I got this itch to do something

But I don't know what.

I want to go here and there

But my wallet says I am not going anywhere

So now all I can do is sit

And watch the time pass me by

Wishing I was swimming or beaching with my buddies

Wishing I can go spend guilt free at the mall

Wishing I had friends or relatives to drive by

But for now I will enjoy my house and my dog

Which is worth more than new clothes and a suntan.

BEWARE

I have a story that I must tell

My soul stirreth uneasy and a tiny troll with red eyes dwell

He's lived in me since I talked with God

Who told me the righteous path is where I should trod

You've been spared death and left here to remain,

but my life's looking glass is one red stain!

I cannot free the troll who pulls my mind towards death

I choke and smother with every breath.

I want to exhume my soul from burden

And this is one life's goal that is certain.

If it takes my last breath I will succeed

To beat the devil with my souls deed.

I will rise above the dark shadows and clean my soul

Because the devils dance has taken its toll.

I will not walk a black shadow of fear and depression

My life is much better and should not be in regression.

I have to work with my God and make the troll move OUT

So I could stand back on the path and follow life's map on God's route.

Be well, fight and pray to God every night.

and curse that troll with all my might!!

I MISS MY DADDY

I cried for my father today

-the good one

I almost hit a car in the parking lot; my eyes were so full of tears.

I heard an oldie on the radio and it took me back to my early years

When you played that song we danced and laughed! You know I loved that song and whether we were in the car or in the house you would always turn it up for me.

I cried for that memory

I cried for that person

-the good one

You left me at age 16

I have not been to your grave in 15

Sometimes I loathe you

Sometime I miss you

I wish my kids knew you and you could play with them and rough house. I know you would spoil them rotten. I can picture you and the boys playing but you fucked things up!

At times I miss you so damn much I want to scream-so many missed memories, conversations and times being together.

-with the good one

Remember when we use to walk on the pier? You'd smoke and I would dream looking at the city sky line……

I carry a picture of you in my heart

You and me.   I was 16 before the other you took you away. You were so lost.

I cry as I write and think of that picture

You still there posing, smiling

Father, daughter-friend-protector-mentor-cheerleader-proud- glad to be able to be there with me, near me. I hate to say it but I love you daddy. I love the good one before you lost it all completely.

The smart one, the poetic one, the one that made Donald Duck voices

Even though there are times I would take any daddy just to be a daughter. I still have a place in my cold heart for you. I wonder how you would have been as we progressed in years and milestones

I see you in my son. The Lord has done it for some reason; I believe it is that he does not want me to bury your memory. I need to remember you-the good stuff. Without you there would be no me, no wonderful children to remind me of whom I came from, who I am and why.

THORACIC THROWBACK

As I lay on a pillow soaked with tears I mourn
I mourn the 24-year-old with a full heart which has eclipsed
into a frigid one
I have the memory of being awakened during surgery and
told, "I am so sorry-so sorry" and waking up not being able
to speak on a ventilator. Days passed and another surgery,
lying in bed for weeks, not being able to stand. I recall a
special table that helped me up as I 'stood'.
Doctors pressing my stomach and feeling pain, having air
in my lungs and being avoided by someone who was
supposed to protect me-which was his oath. He just
slandered my body with a scalpel.
I am angered no one fought for me while I grieved my
injured soul. I am angry at my mother for not being 100%
and leaving major life changing decisions to me. Not suing
that butcher on my behalf.
Responsibility I could not shoulder and now deeply regret.
I was shit on without the power to fight. I chose to grieve
and needed you to fight for me. To get HIM but it did not
happen and I feel repercussions deep within that may never
heal. I am living in a hell of anxiety because I chose first to
heal physically and mentally while shouldering
decisions…decisions…decisions. Someone could have
fought that monster for me. Speak for me when I did not.
Maybe that is why I am so controlling and over bearing at
times now.
That experience has weakened me, beat me, humiliated me.
When I healed and could fight it was too late and all I could
see was him in his scrubs looking back smiling walking
away without knowing…

I panic because I have lost that control
I panic because if I fell no one will be there to catch me and
if they are, can I trust them to hold me?
I panic because no one is looking out for me 100%
100%

LITTLE HELPER

Sometimes it is hard to help yourself by helping someone

My lows can help someone have highs

Thinking about some of what I have been through brings tears to my eyes

Yet someone else can see it as strength

I don't get it

I am still trying to find the good out of someone's self-destruction, medical negligence

and death

the questions are obvious but answers still cloudy

God let me live

that should be enough but it is not

I am searching hard blinded to the answer in front of me

as I dig deeper for a definitive answer

I have got people to save

after I fix myself

ASYLUM

Have you ever felt like you have lost your soul?

Signed a certificate and gave yourself away not knowing you would lose your identity?

Did you ever feel that you could depend on no one for your sense of strength only to forego all restraints?

I have lost myself and do not know where to find me.

I cannot remember what I wanted or was too blind to see what the consequences were.

I never thought I would lose myself but I did.

I lost my passion. What was it?

I lost my independence.

I lost my spunk and zest for adventure.

I am boring.

All I ever do is live in fear, dependence, guilt, resentment and shame.

This is not the woman/wife/mother I set out to be.

I feel beat down by my own negativity.

I feel like someone I did not want to become.

I move one step ahead only to be pushed 100 steps back, yet I try to remain positive and keep going. I am ready to give up.

Who is to blame? Is it all me? My false perception of reality? Am I cut out for domestication?

I do not know what or whom to hold on to in order to keep striving, to go on.

I have gains yet I feel I have nothing to show as a person.

My view.

My poor distorted view.

What do I need to fill my cup of passion, my spark, my zest, my energy?

Why do I feel so beat down, restrained and helpless?

My God please wrap your loving arms around me and strip this beast within me.

I want to breathe wholly and live lively and happily without contempt.

BIRTHRIGHT

"I feel so ugly" I said

"My body feels blah" I mentioned

"My eyebrows need to be waxed" I huffed

"Why did I cut my hair?" I complain

"People may say she is not attractive" I feel

"They will say what is up with that face, she looks mean" I imagine

"She looks tired" I retort

"Hmmm…. "she says looking awed. "I think you look elegant. I think you are very attractive."

"Wow!" I think

I stand taller; I smile within, "*I think you look elegant*" echoes as I gaze into the mirror. I want to see myself now. Simple beauty.

Tired eyes

    Full lips

        Dry face

           Short afro

              looks elegant

somebody can see past the mask of unhappiness and see………ME

WOMEN (at the doctor's office)

Tammy sits and smile in my face
Then talks about everyone who comes in the door
Humph…wonder what she said as I returned my forms to the receptionist
Tammy talks about me, her, her and her, the doctor and her place of employment. So unhappy yet she woke up to grace us with her indignant presence
Tammy is the "I can't do wrong, everybody else has flaws; look at her clothes, hair, make up, this person is a trip" sistah!
She sits there with her dark glasses on, hair as high as the everglades so she can be noticed yet she wails, "What are you lookin' at?" when someone looks at her
You know Tammy is a trip! Instead of talking about the doctor's way of packing people in her office and what she does; why don't Tammy become one and be different? I am sure she can come up with excuses not too. Plays like she gets all A's and was valedictorian but her transcript says otherwise yet she fucking knows it all, thinks she is jack of all trades, but she's just a master of mouth!!
I cannot stand people like her yet I fell into that trap once. I remember I used to be like her because I was surrounded by girls with no self-worth and yet I wanted to fit into their world. I would talk about people like they did me, to get laughs, to be accepted. I fell into the worthless trap and I did it for power; to make someone feel beneath me
Women; no matter how beautiful or educated, we are always made to feel beneath someone. Always comparing, staring, snaring and degrading someone, we feel we must criticize to feel worthy
Tammy is a trip! You go girl!! Go away from me!!

DETROIT

I will always have fond memories of home

I am blessed to leave it and come back to see it through mature eyes

I still get emotional coming home

Home is bitter sweet

Home is dangerous, rotted and lifeless

Home is beauty in the water that surrounds it, the weeping willow that cry for it

So much potential, centuries away from reaching it

I was born there

I know the heartbeat of the city first hand

When I left I missed that heartbeat for I was born there, nurtured there, found and married my love there, I came out of my shell there, I lived one of my lifetime wishes there

so many laughter, so many tears

I never want to live there again but I feel so good when I am there at places that still stand for the way it makes me feel

It is where I began

Hate Therapy

I hate my father. He was a womanizer

an abuser to his wife and children

an all and all egotistical alcoholic jerk

I have a half-brother and can imagine how many more half siblings I have, how many women called my mother telling her of their impending children, how many secrets she holds of the past that she'll never tell.

The times mother packed us up to leave and we would pass you sitting in the living room in your yellow robe, gun in hand. Great family times when grandmother would visit marred by you pounding moms head on the floor, the bruises, the black eyes...

I found out some disturbing things about my father today that sealed the envelope of malice I have for him. I can honestly say I hate the man, the abuser, the alcoholic, the violator, the womanizer, the dreamer, the loser...

He makes me get on God's nerves because I have to ask him over and over to forgive me for my ill will feelings to him

I have forgiven him but I still can't stand his ass! The thought of him makes me want to spit! He had it all but it was not enough. What was he looking for? What was missing? How was he brought up because all of his brothers were not nice to their women, wives to them was like a scratching post to a cat!

Can't say I wish you weren't born because I would not be here

On Father's Day my son says too bad you can't call your dad and I said hell has no phone lines!!

Friennabee

She doesn't want be your friend

She just wanna know your business

What you do for a living, your pedigree, she believes all the gossip from the grapevine not from the direct source even though she talks to you

She smiles in your face then turns directly into a venomous Columbo

Friennabee's always think you have more than them and feels the need to keep you in your place not realizing we all have a struggle. Friennabee's wannabee socialites, be the "IT" person everyone comes too, wannabee town crier, the most popular. She's got her eyes out the window with gossip irons in the fire. I bet she googled the whole neighborhood. Don't be a force against her, she'll turn everyone against you and think you will have no friends

She thinks that is power but I'll surrender to her when Satan is skating down the cul de sac

She thinks you need and want to fit in, your life will be nothing if you aren't in "the circle". She has no clue no one could care less about her let alone the circle of unhappy, nosey, cackling hens with out of control, arrogant children. Ohhh…yeah I want to be a part of that!

I'd rather be the outcast she wonders about, the one she'd rather be about

A METAPHOR

It's funny the reasons why we hide from the essence of who we are

simple statements make you wonder how others see you

why does it matter anyways?

I see me as me. How, now, brown cow

Others see me as the sun, I deny

I used to want to be the sun

it would bring me luck in life and in love now I am older it does not matter; my standards have settled, self-esteem humble, au lait, espresso, latte, charcoal

I realize that how others viewed me, bugged me especially when I was asked about my lineage

stunned me but I could not deny who I am. I love me.

I am invisible.

Tainted Blood (relative)

You left me for him?

He is not around anymore is he? How many have taken his place over and over? Yet you left me for him!

He was the catalyst for your departure unbeknownst to me you harbored a stank resentment of me. You knew your flaws and lowered sense of self when it came to men but when I held the mirror to your face you hated me for it and went to him to solve your esteem issues along with your bottle of Merlot. He could make you feel validated, beautiful, loved, smart, grown up as he screwed you and you played house. Your body deserves it right? I mean, those chronic infections from him means he's giving you the gift that keeps on giving. Better than earrings huh? You could not abstain to heal your heart, you had to keep showing you are special or he'd leave or doubt your sincerity. You had to fill that need at whatever cost and you gladly ping ponged impurities for simple pleasures-I bet it wasn't pleasurable but keep telling yourself that o.k.?

It doesn't matter that he shows you that you aren't the permanent one in his life; you are just the one he calls for a limber experiment. You tell yourself you got this and know his game but can't admit you <u>always</u> lose. Maybe you like things like that but when I hint that you deserve better, it is not allowed. The resentment of me wanting you to have a real relationship was too much for you to bear and you left me for him. It's fine but it is a shame that is what you want for yourself. I still love you but you do not love me. That strong need to belong in the arms of someone who will never want you is much more appealing and important in your life. I hope that you keep the blinders on and avoid other issues you may have.

You've taught me to let others fall and ignore them when they ask for help. You taught me women don't need to know the truth when asked; it is too much for them. You've taught me lessons about the closeness of family and that family should keep their opinions to themselves, friends are fit to understand you better as a person. You never turn the switch and cut your "friends" off that would hurt their feelings. I get it now....

Family equals yes men
Family does not equal opinions and honesty
Family does not equal guidance and good wishes

I hope he makes your vision clear of who you want to be.

Bless her heart

I wish I could pray like my great aunt

I pray in my head silently, rarely fall to my knees

It did not matter what position she was in, she could get down and dirty into prayer

That is why I called her when I needed to fight the devil

"Girl, sometimes I get my broom and sweep that devil outta here! get thee behind me Satan!"

I told her I wish I could pray like her. Sometimes after she begins with Heavenly Father, she'd begin to tear and cry as she laid down her words and no matter what my problem was I would feel better. As I hung the phone on the cradle I always wondered how I can have that effect for myself.

"talk to the Lord like you talk to me! people think I am crazy because I go around talking to him all day"

I feel funny with my attempts at prayer. Does that mean I am not saved? not quite sanctified? I want to be able to cry or speak in tongues when I pray like she did, sometimes I felt that if I did not do those things God would think I am not serious. My aunt was a soldier in Christ!! She made me feel at ease that my way of praying and spiritual balance was between God and I and not a show, I needed to relax and not try so hard for he is my friend, my BFF!

I miss those days of prayer together

Alzheimers torn us apart and I am forced to be without her mind, her words, her stories, her blessings, her honesty, her encouragement

Lost in a world of confusion

"Heavenly father, please watch over my aunt and hold her mind in your hands. Bless her heart- Amen."

Never knew love like this

I never knew love was supposed to sting

Is love about being selfish? color-less? Manipulative mess?

I write this for a friend who is walking around torn up inside

I write this for a cousin who is dying to be accepted by their own blood

I write this for a lover who has a family but feels so alone

They claim they can take it, lying to themselves. If they could take it, meaningless words would not hurt so much, would not sting so much, and would not send their minds into a ball of self-doubt searching for an infinite perfection that still won't satisfy those they want acceptance and love from.

I despise them, those people that hurt my friend, cousin and lover! Those people are not worthy of love from themselves or anyone. Those people are clueless as to how to love. Those people envy and try to destroy and have no inkling of how to love. They'd rather buy love and wear it when necessary for them or for show.

Unfortunately, my friend, cousin, lover is still seeking acceptance, a presence, a pat on the back; every day is judgment day or time to pay up. Sad thing is, everyone feels bad for them except them. They feel bad treatment is the norm yet they know it is not but they still reach out and reach out and get dogged and dogged.

It is hard to watch but all I can do is shake my head and be there for them as they continue to accept mental abuse. At least they are happy.

I write this for a friend who needs to release their inner turmoil

I write this for a cousin who is so unhappy they're only solace is work

I write this for a lover whose family needs to see their strength and not criticize their past weakness.

If they could just be happy

abuse

I lived in fear from the sounds heard in my ears

My life was a fortress from all of our inner house mess

In my room I was safe

I wanted to seal myself away from the screams, the slaps and pounds from a loser who lost all hope

A loser who had a hopeless life trying to have control over a strong wife

A loser with son who was better than he was

A loser with a daughter who secretly loathed him

A rock star, a hero fallen from his self-imposed grace in his own home

I just wanted to stay in my room to escape the sounds of giving up while growing up

Summer thoughts that pass in the breeze

I think of you

summer day

warm breeze

Walking beneath the willow tree

at that tree a robin sings

The seal of a kiss sends off hearts wings

Sitting atop a rock viewing the water

I contemplate thoughts of my mother

I'm spoiled by your love

invidious thoughts but

I'm still your little girl

walking barefoot

in dew grass

I have no regrets of my tattered past

Sitting at the wheel of my car

the smell of summer takes my mind far

I close my eyes and rejoice at this life

If anything is better send me that treasure and

compare it to this bliss!

Walking in the street barefoot on a hot summer night

I'd live in this warmth year 'round without a fight

Another Ex (pression)

I feel if I stay I may kill myself. I am not myself.

I need to kill who I've become, kill the noise of blame. I need to become the old hateful me. Since my Ex liked being treated shitty maybe I should join the band wagon.

You respect those who manipulate you. I should become self-absorbed and dismiss you; maybe you'd like that but that's not my style!

Maybe we have grown apart, separated mentally, our distance has made me distant! Resentment has gone as far as it could go. Thing is......you don't care!

You've seen me hurting, crying, yelling and maybe you like it. Showing that part of your selfishness to keep me fretting since you aren't doing a damn thing to make it better, all you do is push on and do your thang!

How am I supposed to continue to love you, make love to you, want to be near you and build a future together with you?

If I leave I will miss what I had *thought* I built with you but will feel better because I'm forced to have my own damn back! I will be forced to satisfy and love myself again since I am alone with you in my life anyways.

You were supposed to love and cherish me.

Right now I tolerate and wonder.

I wonder why I tolerate the disrespect and your denial.

I am not authentically me.

The resentment started when my feelings were put aside; my wants were just as important as yours. I told you I would feel that way but you didn't hear me.

For months our love has self-destructed on many levels. You denied it, I buried it as we became a tidal wave of doubt and depression.

One such friend

I like me. Others don't.

I don't care why but it seems people are turned off

In their eyes I am too quiet,

> too prissy

> too bourgeois

> too phony

> I smile too much?

I am different and who wants to be common? Although the needy brash people have all the friends

I've scaled back who I am with people. People are people and why should I give my all to those who are just pit stops in my life?

I remember all I ever wanted was friends, friends, friends people to validate my coolness. After having friends, friends, friends I don't know what I was thinking about. Friends have been nothing but disappointments in my life, unexplainable fools! Now I associate with folk on a light basis, I don't get closeness nor do I give it. I am trusted yet I trust no one.

It would have been nice to have someone around for 20 years whom I could talk to without comparison and envy, someone not afraid to tell me things honestly and not get offended or run away.

I have my quirks but don't we all? No one can see past themselves unless it helps their agenda and I am supposed to like that?

I miss my grandma

I miss my grandma
The Neutrogena soap bar smell of her
The Bergamot smell in her hair
her hair- oh how I love to comb her beautiful, long, fine,
pepper grey hair.
I miss her hands and short fingers making rice pudding,
eating Stella Doro breadsticks, creating crafts of dogs and
Christmas wreaths of LOVE and ceramic DREAMS
the excitement of her at Christmas
her 'dancing' that looked like exercise
shopping in the petite department
Her love was infinite and strong
her heavy hands whipped my butt over her petite knees
I long to sit next to her as
…she withdraws on a Parliament cigarette
…she straightens her glasses
…I pick the hairs off her chin
…I hug and smell her
I long to hear her voice sing as she answers the phone
I miss hearing her snore as I walked into her room
I miss her so much I see her in everything lately

I wish she could see her great grandchildren and me

I just want it to be me
and her in the chair
while I comb her long grey, fine hair

Double exposure

What's the life lesson you learned today?

I learned FEAR of self is the phrase of the day

I learned that I can scare myself and ruin my health

I learned anxiety comes in the form of different storms

It makes you dance to irregular beats

And climb many mountains you know you can't defeat

> My arms and legs feel weak
> My stomach is knotted
> My vision is distorted
> My breath smothered

My lover hovering wondering, WHO is this?

I learned that I am not confident

The lesson: I am weak

"Accentuate the negative with a positive"

There is nothing positive about
> wanting to die so it can end
> of strategizing the survival of my loved ones
> of living in fear of something not real
> of driving myself crazy

for attention-*that's wicked*

for the sense of security and being taken care of

for having someone constantly around

because I do not like being alone

I lost myself in a tornado of heresy

I am confused

Who are you trying to be?

What are you learning from your insanity?

Take this anxiety and shove it

I was ashamed to say it
but I wanted to end my
life to set you free

I am ashamed to say it
but this demon had taken over me

I am ashamed to admit
I feel like a lazy mother

I am not who I want to be

I can't find the wife, person
I used to be

Grief has taken my sexuality

I live in a poisoned reality

I wonder how I can raise a family
having a mind as an anomaly

I want to change, to grow, to vibe

Be someone my children look up to
Instead of mommy is sick again

My husband wants to be next to me without feeling I am
another person-a weak nemesis

I want to have no fear and be the rock of this foundation
not living in trepidation

I hate myself

My shame varies in range I am ashamed of being ashamed

I was not raised to be like this

I am NOT this

Fight the fear
Fight the fear

33, where are we?

It is my birthday and I am not glad

It is my birthday and I am sad

No cards, no gifts, no splurges

Just a day of the usual

I don't want a huge fuss just a lot of calls from invisible friends

Packages coming in the mail

Knee slapping birthday cards

And homemade gifts by the kids

I wanted to wake up to burnt toast and runny eggs and my boyfriend helping with the choreography holding a bag of gifts

It is not even 12 noon and depression has sat in its nest and has me writing this birthday mess

Personal mechanics

I am afraid of **IT**

IT cannot hit me but **IT** can hurt me

Deeper than the words of a hateful foe

I am afraid **IT** will sneak up on me

I hate losing my vulnerability to **IT**

IT haunts me day, night, twilight

I cannot run from **IT** for **IT** lives in me

IT taunts me when I peer into the mirror

Stares at me

"You never needed me; I was put here to make you strong"

But I am a wimp for I fear **IT**

I know at any given second, minute, month, year you can hurt me

So I try not to glide in life

Because I know you will interrupt **IT** with your jostle

And I'll turn into an in home fossil

Because you are **IT**

And I fear you more that I fear GOD

I let you take so much away from me

Because I sense your sanctity

I cannot be too happy because you are with me

Am I having a good time or

Are you setting me up?

Ouch

How does it feel to be ranked 2nd in the person who is to be your "soul mate's" life?

I have to put "soul mate" in quotation because the way I feel, that word is unbelievable. Nonexistent.

I don't feel like a "soul mate"

I don't feel like I am #1

I don't feel necessary

I don't feel prioritized

As time goes by I feel less and less of a person with you.

It was to get better, you 'understood' but your understanding is selfish. Me-less.

For several years I have been a distant second to work, to excuses FOR work, to tirelessly listening ABOUT work. Do you ever wonder how many times I have THOUGHT about leaving?

How it pains me that even though you say you love me, I don't believe it I feel there are other things that are more important than me? How my spirit is crushed because you make NO effort to show me that I am #1 after you've been told that I don't feel important in your life. You think of me and work in parallel. You can't see into me because you go into what work did to you.

NOTHING, NOTHING to show me that I am not a distant second. Your words are lackluster because they've been repeated for years. I feel like a fool. Did I make a mistake in helping you better yourself? It didn't do a damn thing for me!

No time

No time is a killer

No time to play

No time to stare into each other without words

No time for music and sharing, cards and games

I feel so lonely and lost and bitter.

Soul mate. What the hell is that anyway? Someone who knows your thoughts before you speak? Who bats for you, treats you tender, rubs your neck?

I feel like I can't do anything right or perfect. I do things the wrong way, the long way, I don't feel like we're equal or that we stand side by side.

I feel second best, second rate, and second hand.

Ouch! That hurts me. What cuts the most are things like reminding you several times to do things for me yet a coworker may lose their job and you feel compelled to help them find another job. You do for others selflessly and without hesitation where my stuff is undone. What sense does that make?

Ouch.

Family cum laude

I'm from a small family you know. I used to envy my friend the youngest of 11 because there was always someone around. Someone to talk to, go out with and to help you whenever.
Food was abundant and love was not scarce. The only problem I saw was no privacy. Then I liked being from a small family for that I always loved my space.

Now that I am older I long for what I don't have again, a large family. My small family has dwindled to a population of five with one on the way out. One member keeps himself distant so let's say it is a party of 3.

I look at the grandeur of older black women and yearn for their guidance, wisdom, truth and breadth of them. I have no one now. I long for my youth so I could brush my grandmothers' hair, play dominoes with my great aunt, listen to my uncle's fables. I longed for Sunday, Monday, and Tuesday dinners of homemade meals with love; good southern soul food meals of that generation. Chicken and dumplings from scratch, fried chicken made from the morning's slaughter, homemade cookies and pies only a grandmother could make and sweet buttermilk biscuits....

Family reunions or basement parties you hated to go to but you had to or it was your life! Where you would hear stories of mischief, of how men really courted a woman, learned bid whist, played with new cousins, heard, "you don't know depression…" stories and you get wisdom you never thought you needed until it hits you later in life. I wanted someone to show me how to sew a dress, bake pies from scratch, iron clothes that would make Martha Stewart give a thumbs up, someone to spin tales of wisdom I could pass on to my kids or friends in time of need.

In my small family population, I have uneasiness because folk don't want to be bothered, I'm always being measured, shells not wanting to be broken, jealousy. In time of need, they will be there for me but I still feel alone in their presence. I am crying for a grandmother's love. Moping around for cousins to gab with. A real sense of belonging is what I am looking for. I am far away from my population and if I was near them I'd still feel far away.

 I want what others have. Doing things in the name of family without feeling it is an obligation. Family meals as a tribe are mandatory and looked forward too. All in the name of family honor. I'd rather have people on the outside wishing they had a family life that is like mine.

A tie that binds.

www.ingramcontent.com/pod-product-compliance
Lightning Source LLC
Chambersburg PA
CBHW060403050426
42449CB00009B/1874